Poetic Peace

Rose Marie Grandberry

Published in the United States of America

ISBN 979-8-89395-871-3 (SC)

Rose M. Grandberry Books
222 West 6th Street
Suite 400, San Pedro, CA, 90731
www.stellarliterary.com

Ordering Information and Rights Permission:

Quantity sales. Special discounts might be available on quantity purchases by corporations, associations, and others. For details, contact the publisher at the address above.

For Book Rights Adaptation and other Rights Permission. Call us at toll-free 1-888-945-8513 or send us an email at admin@stellarliterary.com.

♦ DEDICATION ♦

This book is dedicated to all those who read it and discover that they are not alone and that finally someone understands their life's dilemmas. I pray that you will find comfort and inspiration in these words.

♦ ACKNOWLEDGEMENTS ♦

God is my rock and my salvation. He gave me this gift of words to share with others. It took a while for this to fully develop from within. I've always had a joyful side, never realizing that there was something deeper to be shared with others.

I'm thankful for my daughter Dawanna Davis. She has always been the ideal young lady that I raised.

I send my love to my grandson Xzavier Hamilton, who is the best grandson a Granny could hope to have.

To my niece Janice Allen, I say thank you and I love you. You put this fire under me when your book was published.

Reaching Out

Why Care?

Do we really care about others as we could?
Or do we say,
"I'll just keep to myself as I should?
I don't get involved with the problems of others.
I don't know them. And after all, they are not my brothers."

Thinking like that is very selfish.
It never helps anyone, no matter what the wish is.
Help and good advice are all we can give.
Doing for others makes life easier to live.

We share this entire world with strangers.
Just imagine what would have happened if Jesus never laid in that manger.
I know the world seems to be in disarray.
But things can change from this to that in less than one day.

We all seem to be in such a hurry.
Makes no difference what it is or what we do, we still find time to worry.
We all know that we can be better than what we are.
So peel off that old attitude and try something new.
You may just like yourself a lot better than you currently do.

Helping each other is what God wants us to do.
We'll never know when one day we'll need someone's help too.
Please don't ever think you can do everything all by yourself.
Even a rich man has to depend on someone else for help.

A good pat on the back is a show of gratitude.
But don't let it go to your head and change your attitude.
We all like to be commended for what we say or do.
Just remain humble and thankful, and better days are ahead for you.

So let's try to be a help to someone else, and do for others as well as ourselves.

Where is the Love?

Where is the love that is embedded within our souls?
Does it still remain with us as we grow old?
Do we spread it around as we know we should?
Or do we tell ourselves it won't do any good?
Giving of one's self to another in love is what God is looking for us to do.
He gave us all the love He had within, to spread from me to you.

Now, I realize that it may be hard for some of you just to give a smile.
Love is inside of us all. Start giving in after a while.
You will begin to feel a lot better about yourself.
Soon you will be asking,
"Do I have any love left?"
We will never run out of love; it is replenished each day.
God makes sure that we have enough to give away.
He expects us to pass on that which He gives to us.
Doing this lets Him know that in Him we trust.

So quit being hard-hearted and shutting others out.
It's the life you live that we all care about.
Start spreading your love as thick as can be, and you will see the difference it will make for the whole world to see.

After all we say and all we do, having love and not giving it doesn't help you.
So continue to spread that love around.
You'll be amazed at the ones it will help when they're feeling down.

Passing Time

As I sit and watch the time pass by,
I often ask myself the question why.
Why do we look for gratification from man, when all he can do is
say a few words and give a shake of the hand?
We all seem to want to be put on a shelf, being able to look down
on someone else.
We are all human and should be treated as such.
Although there are times we will wonder just how much.

We carry ourselves as if not to care, when we don't take the time
to even comb our hair.
We wear our bed clothes out in the street, thinking to ourselves we
really look neat.
That may be a trend started by someone else, but you can end it
for yourself.
It was started by one person and I know that's true.
But it can end by one, and it could be you.

It's easy to take a ride, going nowhere.
You'll only be going in circles, never getting you there.
I don't understand why negative actions get so much attention.

Everyone jumps on board with just one mention.

If positive actions could be as strong, all of these negative things wouldn't have lasted as long.

Perhaps one day we'll wake up and see, then realize that this doesn't have to be me.

I'll change my outlook to a new frame of mind and leave all the negative thinking way, way behind.

Hug Someone

Has your body ever yearned to just be hugged, not because of lust,
but just for love?
A hug can help make one's day.
There are times when a hug is better than words to say.

A hug can dry the tears from a child's eyes.
Just getting a hug can really make you smile.
A genuine hug is the extending of a person's arms.
It is intended to give comfort and never to bring harm.

We'll say "I love you" a hundred times a day and hardly give it
another thought when that person goes away.
I find myself in need of a hug from a good caring man, one that
knows how I feel and will understand.

I realize that there are all kinds of people in this world today.
Perhaps I'll get that hug as I continue to pray.
So the next time you feel like you're having a bad day, remember
to keep your eyes and arms open for that hug that's coming your
way.

I Wonder

I wonder, I wonder what could this be.
I feel so empty inside, and that just isn't me.
My head says one thing and my heart says another.
Which one to trust, for there is no other.

I know that this is only temporary, but how long will it last?
I need to settle it and make it my past.
The more I follow my head, the more my heart aches.
And the more I follow my heart, the more my head aches.
I need this to be fixed so I can catch a break.

Will these two parts ever agree?
I certainly do hope so, for this is killing me.
They both had ample time to make this right, instead of a tug-of-war that led to this fight.

I'll go to whom I should have talked to at first, that being almighty God.
He'll settle this dispute because for Him, it's not hard.
He'll remove all of my aches and pains.
I only need to pray to Him and call His name.

So when this same thing happens to you,
just do what I did and He will see you through.

Life

Aging

Age is the one thing that remains a factor in all our minds.
It will creep up on us sooner than we realize, leaving the younger
years far behind.

Take the young woman with her shapely body and fine figure.
When that changes so drastically, she asks herself,
"Who pulled that trigger?"

Then there is the young man who has a fine physique and a full
head of hair, only to look up one day and find it's no longer there.

Time usually does this to all of us.
It is the one thing that changes, because aging is a must.

It is a blessing to live to a ripe old age.
We can look back on our life as being on stage.

We should thank God for everyday of living, for it is because of
Him that this life is given.

Doubt

As we go through life on whatever route, how often do we let that journey become weighed down by that word called doubt?
It can make you second guess your very soul, while trying to remain vigilant and in control.

Doubt steps in whenever it can.
It has been known to rattle the nerves of many a great man.
I was so sure of myself when I started out.
Then somewhere along the way, I picked up that word called doubt.

It will stay with you and never leave your side.
I regret having picked it up while on my life's ride.
How long will I continue to let this anchor dominate me?
It's making my eyes and my mind cloudy, until I can't hardly see.

Doubt tries to convince you to give in by saying,
"Why keep on trying? You can't ever win."
Stand up to doubt and push it aside.
It will try to overpower you when you let it ride.

Remember the next time you meet this word called doubt again,
stand up straight and with conviction say,
"Go on your way, for you are not my friend."

Today's People

As I watch the people of today, I ask myself what's really going on?
Things have certainly changed— some for the right and some for the wrong.
Nevertheless, where does one really stand?
Is it with the right or with the man with a gun in his hand?
I try to evaluate and to get a sense of all this mess.
I'd really like a reasonable answer to this.
I'm perplexed.

I, as well as you, see the boys and men with their pants so low, just one more inch and they could touch the floor.
Oh, they wear them like a badge of honor or being cool, but in reality, they look like today's new fool.
No one wants to see your very behind.
Is this a sample of what's really on your mind?

Young ladies, I see you with these very males.
Your taste is so shallow, and with them you will fail.
Be a nice young lady and don't settle for less.
Raise your standards up above all the rest.
Go on with your life and leave your sorrow with the person who tried to bring you down with no hope for tomorrow.

I speak to all males who have taken a part in this disgraceful display of your body parts.

So let's stop this and start a new trend, and bring back respect to all our men.

Time

Time continues to pass, as it should.
There are times in which, if possible,
I would slow it down if only I could.
I have my reasons for thinking this way, but when reality sets in,
I know that I don't control not even one day.

My heart still aches from time to time.
I know that God is keeping me close as I still have you on my mind.
Time that has passed is only a reminder of yesterdays and yesteryears.
It will cause us to doubt and to face our fears.
We are to learn from mistakes or decisions made in times past, some of which will change our lives for the good or bad. Whichever comes first or last.

I know that we all have some regrets to live with in these present days.
In seeing our life as it is, do we intend to change our ways?
Some decisions we've made can't be changed, and time doesn't always allow us the ability to rearrange.

Wasted time could be considered as a sin, for during that time, nothing was accomplished from the beginning to the end.

So when you see that time has slipped away, just remember to thank God and ask Him for another day.

What If?

What if we looked at our lives as they are today?
Would we be pleased with it or would we say,
"I haven't done as much as I wanted to do.
Is it because of me or because of you?"

What if life didn't have any crooks, curves or turns?
Would we be any better off from the lessons we've learned?
Nothing is perfect, as we all know.
These are the things we deal with in life to help us grow.

I know not why it's so hard to understand why we always think
it's caused by the other man.
Many of us live our lives like an open book.
Some people will stop to read us and others will pause and just
take a look.

Only those that show true concern will try to help.
They try to encourage you to get a hold of yourself when your life
seems to be torn apart.
Accept the aide that a caring person gives to mend your heart.

Pain, for one reason or another, is something we all go through.
It happens to us all, so why not you?
We tend to think trouble and bad times belong to someone else.
It can and will come into anyone's life, despite of ourselves.

So when it seems like the world has let you down, pick yourself
up and wipe off that frown.
The world is here for us all to aspire, but it's up to you to have the
desire.

So put on your wings and get ready to fly.
Just go with it, no matter how high.

Ticks or Kicks?

What is it other than our heart that makes us tick?
Or should I say that gives us our kicks?
Is it that someone that we hold so dear?
Or is it the possibility of losing them that causes us to fear?
Is it the finer things in life that we acquire, then boast to all what you have for them to admire?

Things are just what their names say for them to be.
Things don't jump up and down saying,
"Hey look at me."
We are always looking for something or someone to define who we are.
It's like looking up in the sky, trying to find the brightest star.

Things are only articles in our possession.
It's how we look at owning them that causes our obsession.
We sometimes neglect the basics just trying to stay in the loop.
Saying, "I can't be seen with that!
I'm not of that group."

All we have on this earth is just on loan from God.
He is the one thing that should fill and possess our heart.

Life's Letdowns

What can one do when it seems like life has taken a toll on you?
Do we sit and think about what could be going on, or do we just
ride it out no matter how long?

One's life can change in a mere blink of the eye.
We know not when or even why.
Things will happen in our lives.
Of that, I'm sure.
How do we ease our minds while seeking a cure?

We suddenly become sick when we thought we were healthy.
There is no rhyme or reason.
This includes the wealthy.
There is no way to avoid life's circumstances.
We live from day to day, taking our chances.

Nothing is for certain each day that we arise.
There is always someone or something to bring tears to our eyes.

There can still be joy left for us after going through a storm.
Always remember that God has the last word, as sure as you're
born.

Life offers us so many marvelous things to live for, even though
there are times we don't feel the joy.
We have to put our faith and trust in God to see us through.
He can fix it all and you will feel brand new.

Looking Forward

In looking forward, there is always ground to be left behind.
Remembering this, the future is certainly on my mind.
I can only push ahead and not be led.
It depends on what's inside of my own head.

If we are unable to leave the past without it getting us down, there is no way we can expect to turn our life around.
You see, the past is only good for helping us grow stronger.
It's not worth it to hold on to it any longer.

The past can make us grow hard and cold.
It can stay with us until we're old.
So get rid of it and bury it deep, never to return from an eternal sleep.

Giving up the past can change your whole outlook on life.
Just let it go.
You may surprise yourself in becoming re-acquainted with someone you didn't even know.

Now, the future is new territory yet to be explored.
Just give it your best shot and don't ignore it.
God is there to keep you from falling.
He's holding you up, so just keep calling.
He is the one to answer your prayer.

He was always around when no one else cared.
I'm sure it seemed that He had thrown you aside, but that is never true.
It is from Him that we hide.
The new times coming are really looking bright.
With God by my side, I can truly see the light.

So relax and move forward for what's up ahead.
Remember, we all have a future, and by God we are led.

Don't Listen

I often wonder how could this be that a person can tell you not to serve God—but they can't save me.

No one other than you can save your own soul.
Not man. Let it be your will to serve God and honor Him as best we can.

People have their opinion about most everything, this is true.
Giving into this would be an awful thing, so don't let it be you.

Serving God is the right thing for us all to do.
Don't listen to the person that says it's not for you.
His words are coming from the devil himself.
And once he has you convinced, he'll go on to someone else.

Keep your faith in the one true God above.
He fills our hearts with so much joy and love.
Sure, there will be troubles in our lives as we live.
But there is comfort in knowing that He is always near with peace to give.

Let's do our best to serve God with a positive mind, and don't listen to the ones that the devil is pushing from behind.

Success

Do we always live life the way we think we should?
Or do we strive to make it better if we really could?
There are things that may push us into doing better for ourselves.
We have to get started and stay on track while there's still time left.

Having a good frame of mind is the one thing you'll need.
It will help you reach your goals in trying to succeed.
Success is a gift from God above.
It is given to us because of His never-ending love.

Remember to thank and acknowledge Him in all that you do.
You will find that in doing those things,
He will see you through.
You will always have those who will try to bring you down.
Don't let them get under your skin because of their frown.

Maybe after seeing you succeed in what you set out to do, perhaps they will ask you how and who did that for you.
Just tell them it came from the Lord up above, and anything is possible when you accept His love.

Life Changed

I once thought that I had it all— until I found myself up against
the wall.
My life to me was all I wanted it to be until things changed and all
of my possessions were slowly leaving me.

I asked myself just what was going on?
I'll call and ask my banker for another loan.
The answer I got from him was unexpected.
He said the ones you have are being neglected.

Am I dreaming or is this for real?
I've never been in this situation and I don't like the feel.
Am I losing because I put my success above any other?
That includes my wife, children and my mother.

I thought that living large was something to boast about.
Now I have no one to turn to before being put out.
Who in the world will take pity on me?
After all, when I was riding high and could not see, my mother
always told me to give God the glory.
Now look at the position I'm in telling this story.

We seem to always think the elders don't know a thing.
Just listen to them and see the difference it will bring.
After hitting rock bottom,
I fell to my knees and asked God to have mercy and forgive me please.

He forgave me and now I have a new life.
We're all a lot happier—me, my children, mother, and especially my wife.

Never think that you are in total control.
You could end up like me, falling head first in a deep, dark hole.
Now that my life has changed,
I'm a new man.
No one can do you like only God can.

Remember the Past

When we grow older in our lives, why do we act as though we always did things right?
We all have a past of long ago, but perhaps you choose to forget it, or is that so?

None of us has lived a perfect life.
It was like trying to cut meat with a dull knife.
When we were younger and left home, we did a lot of things that were definitely wrong.

We had freedom that we never had before.
So we did a lot of things after opening that other door.
Let's not try to make the younger generation feel bad.
If only they knew about our young days that we had.

When we were younger, we didn't listen to the elders or anyone else.
It was all about being free and only answering to myself.
After living like we pleased for a matter of time, we finally realized that we were out of our minds.

You can see that we all have a past.
As we think to ourselves,
"That was really a blast!"
It lasted as long as I wanted it to.
But now it's all over. So how about you?

The past is here to keep us strong.
We will forever know the difference between right and wrong.
So when these young people start to spread their wings, just
remember that once we did the very same thing.

So give them as much direction as you can and put the rest in
God's almighty hands.

What is Life?

All lives matter, whether black or white, or wrong or right.
Taking a life shouldn't give anyone pleasure.
It's how we live life that brings the greatest of treasures.

I sit in awesome wonder of all the lives lost to senseless killings.
And at what cost?
To rob, steal and kill is their daily routine.
I've never understood the reasoning or what it means.

What good does it do to continue this trend?
It takes the lives of women, children and men.
We all have to answer to the Man in the sky.
So when you're asked to confess, don't drop your head and
pretend not to know why.

There is a reason for all that we do.
So why not stop the violence?
And let's start with you.

The police are here to serve and protect.
Without them around, we wouldn't give a heck.
There are good police as well as bad.
Let's not put them all down while we are mad.

Please don't judge all law enforcement by the wrong a few do.
Most can be trusted to do right by me and you.
So when being approached by a person of authority, be polite and
cooperate, and become the majority.

What would this world be without their aid?
They have to love what they do, and not just do it for what they're
paid.
So let's stop putting these men and women down, because the
world would be much more dangerous without them around.

When to Say No

When we're trying not to be enticed by people and things of the
world today, do we hold tight or give in because of what they say?
Our steadfast manner is all that we have to help us make the right
decision.
Don't give in because of their sinister criticism.

We can be deceived in a way that says,
"Oh it's all good for you."
But can we believe that to be true?
Whatever you do, don't follow the crowd.
They will take you places where all are not allowed.

You see, being tempted can consume the best of us.
It depends on who we are and what we tend to trust.
We have to be aware of some shiny things.
They aren't all as safe as the trouble they bring.

"Just let me have it for a little while."
They sound as though they were still a child.
"I won't do it any harm.
I'll give it back.
You'll see.
I'll take good care, like it belonged to me."

It has consumed my very soul.
I should have listened.
Now I'm out of control.
Being oppressed by the devil is all that that is.

He wants to possess your life for the rest of your years.
Remember all the flashy things that he said you could have?
Well he'll keep that promise, that one thing is true.
But as long as you're in his grip, he will devour you.

So Sad

As I sit and watch the people of today,
I'm simply amazed at how they act and what they say.
Their thoughts and ideas are very frightening, never listening to
anything that could be enlightening.
Everyone's mind seems to carry evil thoughts.

It makes you wonder what they have been taught.
Even some of the older ones are just as bad.
They probably learned this way of life from their dad.
Where are they headed and when will it stop?
It's like climbing Mount Everest, trying to reach its top.

Sooner or later, this has to end.
We have all lost loved ones and many friends.
No one is willing to settle things without using a gun.
Then after the trigger is pulled, like the coward they are, they turn
and run.
If bullets became obsolete, then what would they do?

I'm not talking about me.
It's all about you.
Everyone believes that they have to get even.
"I will not be disrespected by anyone.
That's why I don't mind packing my gun."

The households of today are really different and will make you
feel ashamed.
The words they call one another makes you wonder if they have
real names.

They call us old school, and maybe that's true.
Take a look at a real man, then take a look at you.
We had then—and still do have—respect for our fellow man.
We said "please" and "thank you" with a shake of the hand.

What have you done to improve the world today?
Not anything at all.
And that's all I have to say.

Eye Catcher

I looked at you as you passed by.

There was something about you that caught my eye.

Your walk was that of a distinguished man, not the walk of a man without a plan.

You seem to be one who knows just where he's going, and not one with no way of knowing.

You see, a confident man is sure of himself, not waiting to be encouraged by someone else.

He pushes himself to be the best he can be.

Surely because he is his own man for the whole world to see.

He will take criticism from anyone else but that's being a gentleman in spite of himself.

You see, being arrogant plays no part in his life.

This is his manner, with or without a wife.

Maybe one day the right woman will come along.

She has to be confident and certainly strong.

Until that happens, continue to walk your walk.

It is so much better than a mouthful of words and senseless talk.

Rules

There are rules in place for every walk of life.
Some we choose to obey and some we say are just not right.
These rules are in place to keep us in line, and once you break them, then that's a rule of another kind.

There are rules for the young and old alike.
There's even a rule for riding a bike.
We follow these rules and never really give them a thought.
There is even a rule for something bought.

I realize that we can't live life the way we see fit.
But some of these rules I just don't get.
I'm sure there is a rule on how to laugh or when to cry, or even a rule on how and when to lie.

There should be a rule on how to wear your clothes and that one would govern us on what not to expose.
There's a rule on the amount of taxes we pay.
That rule will be fulfilled no matter what we say.

There once was a rule on who you could marry.
Now when flying, there's a rule on how many bags to carry.
There's a rule on not to drink and drive.
It's in place to assure that we stay alive.

There's a rule to let it all hang out!
I don't know if I've broken it, since I don't know what it's all
about.

There are many rules for learning to cook.
Please don't forget this one that says when crossing the street, take
a second look.

I know there's a rule for owning a gun.
It's for sure that one isn't followed by hardly anyone.
When we break the rules and lie, cheat, steal and kill, then we've
gone much too far in doing the devil's will.

If only we tried to live close to the rules that God put in place.
In doing that, our lives would be totally changed by God's love
and grace.
There's a thousand more rules that I just don't know.
So I will leave this alone as I turn and go.

So let's try to abide by as many of life's rules as we can, and in
the end we both will become a better woman or man.

Wars

This world has been at war since the beginning of time.
Will we as a people ever choose to decline to settle our disputes
and not be oppressed while constantly trying to prove who is the
best?

Innocent lives are always the ones lost as one continues to ask the
question,
"At what cost?"
The mother that loses her entire family and is left alone with no
one to comfort her and no place to call home.

Enemies can become friends and this much is true when we both
sit down and seriously talk and decide about what to do.
Why waste time fighting one another, as we are all in the eyes of
God each other's brother.

What happened to the saying "forgive and forget"?
All these wars do is destroy lives with little or no regrets.
Time will fix all things if given a chance.
But let's not forget that we'll never know when it could be our last
dance.

Why not reach out to that other country man, the one that is as confused as you and doesn't quite understand.
God isn't pleased with any of this.
Remember He is still in charge and you could be next on His list.

Please let's come together before God comes back to earth.
Then it will be too late to ask what was all of that worth?

Honoring God

Where Were You?

What did you do the day the Lord asked us to pray?
Did you join in or did you turn and walk away?
He didn't command you to do this very thing.
It was for our salvation and the blessings it would bring.
We seem to think that prayer is for someone else.
It works for us all, including myself.

Prayer is a part of talking to God.
No matter how loud or how low, we just have to start.
First we humble ourselves and bow on our knees.
It is in doing this we aim to please.
Simply let Him know what's there in your heart, and given due
time, He will do His part.

Sometimes prayers are answered right away.
Then there are times it will be another day.
Please don't lose hope and go into despair.
Sometimes the darkest hours are when He really cares.
These are not the times we put Him to the test.
He's working and waiting on you to bring out your best.
So whatever you do, don't fail to pray.
Send up some timbers each and every day.
God is listening to everything we say.
I'll say it again and again—don't forget to pray.

My Butterfly Colors

I live my life as being a butterfly, with all my colors in the earth's sky.

Each one is an accent to my wings, never wondering or considering the look of my color scheme.

To soar. To soar.

Never ever are they meant to carry sorrow.

After all, God gave them to me for today and tomorrow.

My life is full of so many things.

My greatest joy is the serenity of my Christian being.

Some live each day as if there's no tomorrow— until death strikes and brings a world of sorrow.

These are the ones that swear they will change, but only for a little while, as sadness remains.

Change is available for all of us.

It's not only a luxury for the ones who trust.

God's love for us is oh so real.

It lives in us all as we choose to feel.

He gives us all the same opportunities to soar or sink, but there is a conscience to answer to, despite what we may think.

I choose to display my colors in the life I live, letting it be known to all that my heart is fulfilled with the love that God placed inside of me.

I can never be as good as He expects me to be.

I wear these colors and soar so high until the tip of my wings reaches heaven's sky.

For one day I'll never again touch the ground.

That is when all of my colors will be heaven-bound.

What To Think

When one is all alone, does the mind tend to wonder?
I suppose it does because of the emptiness we're feeling.
We become self-centered on ourselves, never thinking of anyone else.
Our thoughts become overpowering, as to leave us in a world of pain, forgetting that there is comfort to be had even after a rain.

The mind can take us places far and wide.
It always depends on us keeping a place in our minds for God to reside.
He will stay in our heads and our hearts.
Just open up and let Him in, and He'll do His part.

We can be consumed by His power and His might.
Let Him take you over. It's a beautiful sight.

We are constantly seeking out our friends for advice.
Just give it to Jesus and never think twice.
He will never tell a soul about what was discussed, not like a so-called friend.
On Him you can trust.

After He has given you peace of mind, take Him with you everywhere you go.
Don't leave Him behind.
Go tell the world how good He is.
It will fill your heart with joy for many, many years.

Trees

If I were a tree, what kind would I choose to be?
Would my branches grow so wide until almost anything could
have a place to reside?

My height would seem to touch the clouds above, while my
shadow below would give off that shade of love.
My roots would extend deep into the ground until my thirst was
quenched from the water I found.

I'd stand as erect as God intended for me to be.
After all, I am a tree.
Each day that I stand tall and in place, my leaves keep me covered
as to hide my face.

I'm not the weeping willow that droops and cries.
It has never taken the time to dry its own eyes.
I feel so sad for that tree.
It never lifts its branches to see how happy it could really be.

When the time comes for us to shed our leaves, we give them up
for the renewing that we will receive.
There are so many of us, I can't name them all.
Some grow weak, while others grow tall.

Without any help at all, some take that inevitable great fall.
This tree served its time, giving shade and a place to rest.
It will be a memory for all things that gave them rest.

A tree is more than a place where the birds live.
It supplies shelter for building our houses with the wood that it gives.
Our Lord and Savior Jesus Christ was nailed to the cross from a tree.
I'm saying that's how precious it was to take on the sins of you and me.

So next time, take a long hard look at a tree, and ask yourself what has it done for you and me.

Dreams

Are our dreams the hopes of our life's visions?
Or are they the moments that occur to sort out our life's decisions?
Either way, they make us wonder what they really mean.
We sometimes react to them, even though it's a dream.

Some dreams occur because of what's in our hearts.
Others are because of the life we've lived that has set us apart.
We try to associate what we can remember to anything soothing
to our minds.
But we rarely recall all that happened, so we just leave it behind.

A dream can make you laugh or sometimes cry.
Only the dreamer knows the real reason why.

We also daydream and let our minds wander far and near, yearning
for the answers that would make our life more clear.

Some call that a person with their head in the clouds, never hearing
their name spoken when called out loud.
I suppose that it's okay to fantasize, but waiting on things to come
true can bring tears to your eyes.

We'll keep on dreaming, whether asleep or wide awake, and ask
God for the answer to them all, for goodness sake.

Changes

Change comes in so many forms. We change our minds, our clothes, addresses and countless other things, including our names.
At any given time, none of this will ever remain the same.

Do we make a change because it is the right thing to do?
Maybe deep down inside you're thinking others are tired of listening to you.
When making a change, be true to yourself.
It won't give you satisfaction if you do it for someone else.

Once upon a time, we were all boys and girls.
Now we're men and women facing changes over this entire world.
Just like God changes a caterpillar into a butterfly,
He will do the same for us, on that we can rely.
As sure as we continue to live, some kind of change will take place.
Next time, take a longer look in the mirror and notice the change in that face.

Change from the outside is for everyone to see.
The most meaningful change is the one taking place inside of me.

The change from within alters your soul.
It will make you feel as though you're out of control.
Please don't be alarmed when your heart feels light and your eyes fill with tears.
That is God warming your heart and calming your fears.

From this day forward, your life will never be the same.
You will feel renewed each time you call His name.

Life Without a Head or Heart

Life without a head or heart, for after all, they aren't far apart.
We were born with both, not taking in consideration the condition of either.
The head being the top of the body and the heart is the middle.
Which of these could we live without?

For with the head, we can see, hear, talk, eat, smell and think.
Imagine not being able to do those things.
We could avoid the harsh words spoken, the ungodly things we see, the impure thoughts we have and overindulging on fine foods.
We wouldn't have to pay for hairdos or cuts.
We couldn't be held accountable for our thoughts or our rolling eyes.
We wouldn't have to pretend to be happy when we are really troubled.
After all, no one can see me.

Soon I would be tired of not having a top on my body.
I was given a head of God's choice, with all the necessary parts: a mouth, a brain and a voice.
My head allowed me to look at what God had made for me to enjoy.

My body wondered what is this thing above my shoulders?
It seems to make me think about others and to see the works of the
Lord.

I'm glad to have this head.
It gives me the ability to see the good in my fellow man, and to
give encouragement to others.
Now, how did I ever think I could live without it?
It has changed my life.
Now I can see God's goodness and proclaim Him Lord forever.

Not having a heart, we wouldn't have to feel anything for
anybody.
We could go through life doing as we please, without any
consideration for others.
We wouldn't feel the love of others or the sadness of lost loved
ones, hence no heartaches.
We wouldn't have to listen to that continual beating in our chest
or the times when it seems to run faster or slower than need be.

Oh Lord, why do I feel a void in this body?
Please give me a heart and I will use it for the goodness in this life.
And create in me a clean heart, one that shows love and
compassion, one that will live in the memory of all that I meet.

God, you gave me a head with a mind to see the wonders of your
works, and a heart that is growing closer to thee.
Having these two body parts, they don't always agree.
There are times they fight right inside of me.
There are times one will overrule the other.
Sometimes in a good way, sometimes bad.
It's a matter of doing the right or wrong.

To remedy this, God needs to dwell in both equally.
How is it that warm blood flows through our veins to our heart,
yet we can be cold-hearted to one another?
As I come to the end of this fantasy and take my seat,
I'm thankful for the two things that made my body complete.

Now tell me, was this really as bad as it seems?
For after all, it was only a dream.
In the beginning I had no head to lead me anywhere.
I had no heart, so I didn't care.

Are we ever as good as we should be?
Or are we just putting on a front for man to see?
These things I say to you as well as myself.
Let's get it right before there's no time left.

Transitioning Woman

As I go through this transition in my life, knowing my husband is gone and I'm no longer a wife,
I have a new world to face without him by my side.
I have to conquer this, and not because of my pride.

God gives us all our lives to live, whether long or short, it was the time He gives.

Even though we were a couple and that is no longer true, it will take a lifetime to get over losing you.
Oh I'll be all right because God is keeping me close by His side.
He tells me to hold on and just enjoy the ride.

I can only imagine where this will lead.
But the King is in charge. So for worry, there is no need.
When He thinks that all is well and I'm ready to be let go,
He'll still be around because He loves me so.
His caring for us is all we'll ever need.
Just let Him take control and see how good life can really be.

After all, I went through this transition.
Now take a look at me.

My Quiet Space

There are times when I just like to be in a place where it's calm
and serene. In my own space.
I marvel at the works of my Lord and Savior.
It's His blessings that grant me His favor.
We never seem to get it all right.
After all, we've been given just this one life.

We all have only ten rules to obey.
But they seem to get harder and harder each and every day.
We can only ask God for strength to endure.
This will be a lifelong journey, not a short tour.
Putting God first in all we do is the greatest of these rules for me
and for you.

God gives peace to all of us.
It's inside of our hearts and our souls, no matter how young we
are or how old.
The best place to be is in the arms of the Father above.
He holds us close so as not to escape from His never-ending love.
But if we choose to leave that comfort zone, remember that He is
still with us when we feel alone.

We all say that we need our own space.
But just remember the entire world is free to all and that God owns
each place.

When To Choose

How long do we have to choose the Lord?
The answer is very simple.
It's up to you, for He will not force you to follow Him or worship
in His temple.
We know that He is always here, so we take our time.
Be careful in doing this, thinking that my time is mine.

We all have to spread our so-called wings.
That's how we learn about other things.
Some of us take a lifetime and never get enough.
We'll say,
"I just can't quit doing this kind of stuff."

We know in doing these things, it's terribly wrong.
Perhaps I'll stop before too long.
When we feel that it's time to come in,
God will welcome us, not asking,
"Where have you been?"
No questions asked; never reminding us about our past.

Our lives are forever changed by the wave of His hand.
We are safe and secure because He's in command.
After taking a hard look and assessing your past, be forever
thankful you realized it wasn't meant to last.
You see, in telling the crowd that you believe in the goodness of
God, maybe they will try Him too.
It's not that hard.

A Day Without Jesus

Some tend to think that they can live without Jesus in their life.
Perhaps that's the reason for all our trouble and strife.
Our world is filled with many enticing things.
They look good, but think about the trouble they bring.

Oh we'll say,
"One time won't hurt to try."
But that's the devil talking and you know it's a lie.
It is his duty to deceive us and make things look good.
He believes that he can do all things, just like Jesus could.

He makes everything seem like the best there is— until after you
try it and your world turns to tears.
Oh let him go on his merry way.
You don't need him to comfort you on any day.

He will continue to come by and knock on your door.
Simply tell him,
"I've got Jesus. What do I need you for?"

Jesus is all we ever need.

Let's get on our knees and call on Him.
He'll take us back in spite of any of them.
God knows our hearts from beginning to end.
He is the best one to call when needing a friend.

Relationships

Living a Lie

I can't believe after all these years,
I'm left to cry deceitful tears.
You painted a picture that I never knew.
It wasn't for me, but all about you.

I will forever be amazed about the lies you told.
Tell me how you could be so brazenly bold.
I'm constantly reminded by your friends of the way your life was
in place to face your eventual end.

I never know just what to expect.
I'll just wait to see what will be next.

Why do men have to tell each other lies?
It never accomplishes much. It's only a disguise.
Now I'm left to sort out this mess.
I have to succeed, for this is my test.

I will not desecrate your memory because of your ego.
That's the way men talk when trying to be the hero.
We women are always left in the dark.
It's sort of like fenced-in dogs waiting to see which one will
bark.

For whatever reason, they do these things.
I suppose it's because only angels have wings.
If you have to tell lies in order to get attention, then that's really sad and there's nothing more to mention.

So try to be as truthful as you can be, and you will still have friends.
Just wait and see.

No Longer a Home

As I enter this house all alone,
I realize this house is no longer a home.
This is where my husband and I lived.
We shared this place for many years.

Now that you're gone, it's not the same.
It seems like the walls call out your name.
We shared so many happy memories in this place.
Now it seems to have lost its joy, and now it's just space.

I know that the Lord called you away.
But we are never ready for that eventual day.
We were together longer than some people live.
That's why I wonder what's left to give.

I will continue to go on and be the best I can be because I know
that's what you wanted for me.
I'll carry you in my heart wherever I go because I know that you
loved me so.

We often talked about that eventual day when one was left and
the other passed away.
Well, that day has come for me and for you, but that doesn't
make it any easier to do.

These are the times your life is turned upside down.
I'll make it through because Jesus is still around.
He wipes away those lonely tears and comforts me while I face
these newfound fears.

Holding On

Why do we tend to hold on to a relationship that isn't meant to be?
We continue to hope that it will change, while keeping our eyes
closed, refusing to see.
A one-way love can tear at your heart.
It will cause so much pain, like you're being torn apart.

You constantly ask yourself,
"Why is this happening to me?
I want and need to be loved.
Don't you agree?"
We'll put up with them and be put down.
It really doesn't matter how we're treated, as long as they are
around.

There are people that will use you when they don't feel the same
as you do.
Start building on being a stronger person until there is a new you.
The old saying says,
"When you find a fool, bump his head."
I have seen the light, and that fool is dead.

We can all be mended from a broken heart.
It may take some longer than others.
Just give it a start.
We never know what the future holds for any of us.
There is God to lean on, and by all means, to trust.

Reasoning

Does two plus two always make four?
What if it was less or much more?
Some things are and will always be the same, but not for us who
desire to change our name.

We know that God made only two sexes, a boy and a girl.
Now some of society says that there is another in this great world.
Those that choose to agree with that while singing that equal song,
they are far off track because God never does anything wrong.

People have and will always try to justify the wrong that they do.
God has the last word in all of our lives, and not me or you.
We will all be judged by the life we choose to live and also by the
ungodly love life some choose to give.

Immoral behavior is spreading wider every day.
There are times I wish I had a magic button to make it all go away.
Sin has been around since the beginning of time.
It all came about when Eve changed Adam's mind.

God sees and knows all that we do.
We should strive to be ready when He says,
"I'm coming for you."

Loneliness

The longest days and nights spent are the ones all alone.
Seems like everyone in the world is doing something, while I'm
sitting at home.
Do they really know that I exist?
Or am I just the one that the world seems to have missed?

I fill my time doing meaningless things.
It never fills my heart with the joy I'd hoped it would bring.
Do I continue to stay inside and entertain myself?
Or do I get out in the world and join in before nothing of me is
left?

I'll try to fit in where ever I can.
It won't be easy for me, so I hope you understand.
I'm gonna drop this old sad and lonely feeling.
It doesn't do me any good, and for that I'm willing.

All of this is new to me, as you can see.
I've never been very confident of myself and this will be hard for
me.
I'll begin by opening up and letting others inside my heart.
I'm sure that when that happens, we'll never be torn apart.

I'm ready to get started and begin to live again.
This was all possible because of a new and good friend.

What's Wrong?

I feel like my life is falling apart.
Included are the things that I hold dear to my heart.
Work is starting to go lacking.
I need to get a grip before they send me packing.

I can't seem to find anything that can bring me out.
I know that there is something wrong and there is no doubt.
Or is it too deep to talk about?

I'm a young woman in my mid-thirties.
I have a few friends, but no true buddies.
I still live at home with just me and my mother.
Could it be that I feel trapped, and could I recover?

I do believe that this could be partly to blame.
She depends on me so much until I feel like I'm going in- sane.
I was born very late in my mom's life and maybe that's the reason
why.
It's as though she is holding me hostage until the day she dies.

I love my mom, and this she should see.
This isn't any good for her or for me.
We really do need to come to an understanding because living like
this is too demanding.

I've tried to cope but it's getting the best of me.
She knows that something is wrong, but refuses to see.
How can I tell her that she is smothering me?
I have a life to live and need to be set free.

I feel as though this will be made right.
I prayed and asked God to fix this when I laid down last night.

Lost Love

Who's to say who's right or wrong, when we've been living this lie for much too long?
We started this relationship many years ago.
Now we're just passing time, waiting to see who will go.

We both know that there's not much left, but we continue to keep quiet while deceiving ourselves.
When the love has dried up and the heart has grown cold, it's hard to admit that it's all over while trying to console.

Either way it goes, we both know that things have changed.
Neither one of us reaches out and calls those sweet names.
We are both hurting deep down inside.
Let's just get this over and save our pride.

We got so busy running here and there, never taking the time to let each other know we care.
Then suddenly one day we looked up and found that we had grown apart.
Now we are wondering what do to with fragments of a bro- ken heart.

When it's over and love has come to its end, just be glad that you
know it and part as friends.
People will say,
"I thought that you two were doing so well.
You both kept it to yourselves, so no one could tell.
It's good to know that the two of you will be okay.
I'll give you both my blessings as you go your separate ways."

Contemplating or Speculating?

I can't seem to concentrate on other things for thinking of you.
I need to get this in check.
But what can I do?
We haven't spoken about a possible future yet.

That may be possible, but on that I won't bet.
We never know what's up ahead.
Is it my heart or my head?
I can't decide.
By both I am led.

I also feel that he wants to go deeper.
He has made sweet comments that have made me weaker.
I won't read a lot into any of this.
Cupid has an arrow, and he may just miss.

I'm very emotional at this time in believing that one day he could
really be mine.
I don't know what's at the end of this road.
It could be a bouquet of flowers or a bucket full of tears.
Either one will dry up after so many years.
Nevertheless,
I'll take my chances and pray for the best.
Who knows how this will turn out if this is a test.

We both may have found what we had been looking for.
If not, we'll just close this open door.
We'll say to one another,
"We really did try," then ask ourselves,
"Was it all a lie?"

Reunited

When do you think of us as being a pair?
Is it when you're all alone and no one else is there?
I think of you all the time, and maybe I shouldn't.
But I just can't help myself.
And if I could, I wouldn't.

It took a long, long time for us to find each other again.
If nothing serious comes of this, at least we can still be friends.
So much time has passed for both of us.
First of all, we have to build a solid connection of trust.

We have both grown from the years that we have been apart, but
we can still feel the joy between both our hearts.
We'll forever wonder about people that we once knew, but all of
that has changed because you found me and I found you.

So let's just get started from here and now.
We need not go too far back in time asking each other how.
Time is just as it is—long behind us for all those years, realizing
that we both still have our doubts and fears.

Only the time we both have left will ease our minds.
After all, we are just a bit older but still good and kind.
We can only speak for ourselves and no one else has a say.
We'll make the best of this as long as we continue to ask God for
one more day.

Losing A Friend

When did the laughter between us end?
Was it when we both discovered that we were no longer friends?
I can recall the times when no one could pull us apart.
People would say,
"It's like they shared the same heart."
I guess that all things will change as time goes by.
It's enough to make you sit down and have a good old-fashioned
cry.

I believed us to be the closest of friends, but these things will
happen when it involves men.
I never thought that you would do this to me.
I've stood up for you and beside you for the whole world to see.

Some men will always make a play for their woman's friends.
It's up to her to stop it before it begins.
Please don't think that you're getting over on her.
Maybe for a while that could be true.
But when you're found out, all eyes are on you.

Now you and he have disgraced yourselves.
You're looking for a friend, and there's no one left.
I'll forgive both of you and wish you the best.
I can go on with my life because I passed this test.

Just be aware that this could happen to you.
There are other women that do what you do.
So if you ever find someone to put your trust in, you'll forever be asking,
"Is she really my friend?"

These are the questions that will remain in your head.
You'll keep asking yourself,
"Was it worth it taking him to bed?"

I Will Not Cry

I will not cry about an old friend that showed up in my life.
If only for a little while, it was pure delight.
We've talked about old times of long ago.
It was good to remember, and we laughed so.

We expected this reunion to go a bit further.
Then we both realized that we belonged to another.
Me to the memory of my deceased spouse, and you to whomever it is in your house.

So we'll just let life continue to pass us by and remember that chance encounter was only to say hi.
So if we happen to see each other again, we both know now that we can only be friends.

♦ ABOUT THE AUTHOR ♦

Rose Marie Grandberry is a woman of joy and laughter. She has worked in many areas of commerce, and has managed a multi-million-dollar company (from which she has since retired).

Rose is a faithful member of her church, and is looking forward to giving poetic peace to her readers.